"1823"

beloved

poems, praise & prayers

jeannine gibson

FREILING
PUBLISHING

Copyright © 2021 by Jeannine Gibson
First Paperback Edition

All rights reserved. No part of this publication may be reproduced, distributed, or transmitted in any form or by any means, including photocopying, recording, or other electronic or mechanical methods, without the prior written permission of the publisher, except in the case of brief quotations embodied in critical reviews and certain other noncommercial uses permitted by copyright law. For permission requests, write to the publisher, addressed "Attention: Permissions Coordinator," at the address below.

Some names, businesses, places, events, locales, incidents, and identifying details inside this book have been changed to protect the privacy of individuals.

Published by Freiling Publishing,
a division of Freiling Agency, LLC.

P.O. Box 1264
Warrenton, VA 20188

www.FreilingPublishing.com

ISBN: 978-1-956267-23-5

Printed in the United States of America

dedication

To the Jeromes in the far-off island nation
Who first told me the wondrous story of
    salvation
To the Cares whose unconditional love caught
    me unawares
To my brothers and sisters in the New Jerusalem
    Community
You are a beautiful part of my history
To those who supported me through University:
Brian, Sherry, Johnny-Do
Loretta, Linda, and Michelle too
To those at the little church in Milan
For your welcome and open arms
To those ministering in the heart of Brazil
During my summer there as a wide-eyed girl

To those I've journeyed with through the long
    and winding way
and in the daily grind of the every day:
Cheryl, Heidi, Laurie, Nancy, Nora, Pam, Sherry,
    Tina
The Jazzergals, Al-Anon, Love Church, and
    Tranquility tribe
You've been right there by my side
Without you I would not have thrived

To my trusted counselor who stated five
    years ago:
"You have something to say,
You're going to write a book one day!"

My Grandma Annie who sacrificed her
    minimum wage to pay for my first flight
For a trip that would change the course of
    my life
To my California family I love from afar
You are my Sun and Star
To my Father whose final words to me were
    "Just Write"
My Mother who has cradled me with care
    and prayer
My love for you is without measure.
You gifted me with siblings I treasure:
Rena and Lisa who have reached the
    distant shore
and are not here with us anymore
Angela, Gary, and Cara Jo:
Your unwavering support is the soil in which
    I grow

To John, my faithful spouse of twenty-five years
Amid less laughter and more tears
We kept our vows through thick and thin
Even when we wanted to give up or give in
To Shayla, Jack, and Joy, Heaven's gift of children
You are my greatest teachers for life lessons

For those I have yet to speak with and meet
May you know Jesus, the ruling Viceroy
Over all of our triumphs and defeats

contents

a miracle in the making 1
a prayer for mothers 3
all mine 5
always angry 6
anthem 9
because of you, mom 11
behind closed doors 13
beloved 15
better than you 16
coffee cup 18
come heal here 19
cry baby cry 21
daughters 23
diminish 24
empty 26
even in babylon 27
fix me 29
forgiveness 31
fought and found 34
fully known 36
gift of faith 37
good news now 39
how do you say goodbye to your mother? 42
i asked you to leave 44
i choose joy 45
i keep remembering you 47
in the grey 49

in the meanwhile 51
last kiss 53
living grief 54
more 56
morning rush 58
on the day i was born 60
outside the gate 62
put the stone down 64
railroad tracks 66
remarkable 68
run into hope 70
sabbatical 71
shoreline 73
stay 75
ten thousand decrees 77
that girl 79
the better part 81
the exchange 84
tired 85
to be vulnerable 87
upside-down 88
waterfall 90
we shared scars 92
what if 95
when dreams sleep 97
wish you were here 99
worlds upon worlds 101
wounded womb 102
write don't fight 103
wrong made right 104
about the author 107

a miracle in the making

I am a miracle in the making
Not quite there but keenly aware
That I am not yet what I am meant to be
This powerful seed is springing up inside of me.

I fall down and I rise again
Cause I am not giving up nor giving in.

The miracle is me.
The miracle is you.

And right now is my best time for a brand
    new view:
To know your love constantly, relentlessly
    pursues.

I will sometimes suffer and often wait,
But you'll see me moving from grace to great.

That miracle to come my way,
In a soon and future day,
Is already in play.

The miracle is already in the making.
Moving me from valley to hill.

For you, Lord, make me a miracle in the making
In every day and in every way.
As I am surrounded by your infinitely good and gracious will.

a prayer for mothers

To touch the Divine
Here on earth
In this place and time

To let go of what she did and didn't do
And anything that keeps her from knowing
    and loving You

To hear your voice
Soft and quiet
Loud and clear
Shouting in her heart
And whispering in her ear

To see your hand at work
To gaze at your beauty
To know this is her joy
And not her duty

To taste of your gladness and goodness
In each gifted moment

To breathe in and out—to stop and smell
The fragrant roses of your perpetual delight
To wonder and to tell
Of this earthly and eternal friendship

To touch Your heart
As she deeply loves and deeply lives

To be at rest and secure
Solid, immoveable, and free
Anchored and unstoppable

To know that her best day is today
Not yesterday nor tomorrow

To let go of all regrets and powerful sorrows
And wallow joyfully in each of her tomorrows

To dance again with the Divine
And let her internal eternally incandescent
    light shine

all mine

The Divine is all mine
Nothing does He withhold from me
He loves me with what is love indeed
He gives to me exceedingly
In every time and for every need
The Divine is all mine

always angry

Always Angry
That's Me

Hurt, scared, much-afraid
Don't touch me. Touch me please.
Don't love me. Love me please.
Don't joke with me. Joke with me please.
Don't be near me. Be near me please.

Bewildered and lonely.
Deep anger. Roaring within.
Tightly holding hands with despair.
Push you away. Please come close.
Push me. Pull you. A violent tug of war.
    Every day.

Nothing you do or say will take this anger away.

It lives there in the heart of an angry child.
Then an angry young woman.
Next an angry wife.
Then an angry mother.

"Why so angry?" you inquire
"You have so much. Look around you."
But anger clouds my view.

"You oughtn't be angry."
Tell that to the child who daily lives in fright.
Who lies in her bed—knowing deeply that
> things are not as they should be, they are not right.
Sneaking down the back staircase to her father
> in the middle of the night.

Pounding on the door, waiting for help.
"I'm scared, Dad. Really afraid of all this living,
> and all this dying."
"You and Mom not really one, wanting to love
> and be loved, always trying."

But not understanding how
I know that now.

And still the deep anger burns away
Each and every day.
Why so angry?
All. The. Time.
Time has not been kind.

You didn't make me the angry person I am
> today.
Mostly, I just came that way.
Packaged up in laughter and smiles.
Untie the tightly wound ribbon, and it all
> falls apart.
To reveal my scared and angry heart.

beloved 7

A chasm of anger between you and I.
Trying and failing, to love and be loved
When this anger stands in my way, our way, each
    and every day.

I have re-created my angry life
as the angry wife.

I thought I left it behind—far, far away
In the yellow house on Tipperary Hill
Running fast and furiously.
But it has caught me still.

And dragged me to the ground
Pounding its uncontrollable fits and fists into our
    marriage and our home.
Crushing what could have been into what ought
    not to be.
Until all that is left is me.

Without you, without us
Angry and alone.
Running down the staircase in the middle
    of the night,
trying to find my way back home.

anthem

Say it and repeat
I am complete

In and of myself
No need to prove a thing to me or you or
 anyone else

From the tiniest of seeds
All I need
Is planted within me
And grows a majestic tree

A beautiful silhouette and form
Withstanding each and every storm
Bark scarred and torn

Weathered arms outstretched
"Batter me with your wind and rain,
 sun and cloud"

Say it aloud
I am complete
In and of myself

For I am deeply rooted in love
Come shelter in my strong branches
Through the dark and lonely night
Take shade from the burning daylight

I am strong
I stand complete
In and of myself
I give and give
And live

because of you, mom

∽

Funny, lively, brilliant that's what you are
Resourceful, persistent, faithful, whether near
    or far.

Because of you—
I love my children, husband—and libraries too!

Because of you—
Puns are much more fun
And I'm always gleaning
For words and their deeper meaning.

Because of you—
I know the Latin root to every English word
And I've secretly enjoyed being a nerd.

Because of you—
I know how to spell, and quite well!

Because of you—
I know what it means to go the extra mile
To be with a needy person or a hurting child.

Because of you—
"Like water off a duck's back,"
I am able to stay on the right track

I don't let what others say
Ruin my day.

Because of you—
I have a constant circle of love—my sisters
    and brother
Best friends like no other.

Because of you—
I understand love and lavish grace
It's all right there, in my mother's face.
All because of you, Mom.

behind closed doors

I stood there in that newly claimed space
    of yours
On your separate floor, outside your door
Wishing you a good night's sleep
Wanting you to let me in
To give me a hope to hold, to keep

But the door stayed closed
And so I stood for several seconds more
Outside the barred bedroom door
Breathing in
Your scent of Irish Spring
Waiting for something
The door to open wide
Longing for you to pull me to your side

As I stood there, slowly breathing in and out
I wanted to shout
"What is this waiting all about?"
You don't know you say
You don't know the way

But I do
It's me together again with you
It's simple really

Don't you see?
It's you with me.
The way it was meant to be.

But you're safe behind that closed door
You don't have to deal with me anymore
With demands, emotions, and tears
With all of the sadness and fears

I want you to be safe with me
Enveloped in our imperfect history

Please come out my heart yearns
But the bridges are all burned

So I go away
Because you don't ask me to stay

beloved

When all other loves fail
I am beloved

When those who promised to stay forever
Cannot weather
Life's storms and gales
I am beloved

When children turn against and rebel
And the forces of evil and hell
Push me to the edge

I fall into the arms that hold me safe and still
For I am beloved

By a love so fierce
It was willing to be pierced

That love will never fail
But shall always prevail

I am gifted each and every day
With a love that knows no bounds
Where I can forever turn and forever be found

I am beloved

better than you

I'm better than you
Because I don't do what you do

I hold the upper hand
This you must understand

I'm head and shoulders above you
In all I say, think, act, and do.

I won't put these well-worn stones down
No. I'll keep picking them up from off the ground

Throwing them straight at you
Because I don't do what you do

Don't you realize
Don't you know
You're half. Not whole.

Not like me at all
Though I hate watching you succumb and fall
A part of me perversely delights in what I see
Because it just goes to show what I know
That I'm better than you. Because I don't do what you do.

I haven't become someone like you
I would never do what you do.

No. I am so much worse
Reciting chapter and verse

Shutting you down
Watching you drown

Just so I can keep my proud place
On this lonely, higher ground.

coffee cup

Morning by morning
I stand in the kitchen
With my coffee cup full

Cold hands clutching my mug
A sad substitute for a warm hug
Sipping in silence
Quietly wishing we were one
That we were whole

The robust black sweet aroma signals a new day
Will this be the morning when we make a
   new way?

My cup is empty now
I want you to fill it up
With kind words, gentle answers, even a touch
But that is asking way too much

So I pour myself another cup
Mixed not with sugar and cream
But with tears and shattered dreams

come heal here

∽

Life hurts, but God you heal.
Come and heal this fractured family, each and every one.
All the wounds, sin, sickness, resentment, doubt, and fear.
Come heal here.
Apply the balm of your mercy, love, and grace
To every hurt and in every place.
Bring healing to wounded souls
Broken minds
Battered hearts
Tortured spirits
So that we are no longer walking lame
In our sin and shame
Bring abundance in our scarcity of grace
Meet our ever-present needs
Feed our starving souls with your everlasting feast of joy
Bring healing truth to the inmost parts
A piercing light into our hearts
Reveal, restore, bring even more
Than what we request
We plead and ask for your very best
To no longer settle for anything less than what you desire
Holy Spirit, inspire.

Bring us to new heights
From this dark, shadowy valley to a shining
 place on your conquering hill
So that we each delight in obeying and doing
 your perfect will

cry baby cry

When you cried
I saw you on the inside

A heart broken apart
Trying so hard to make a new start

You not knowing where to begin
Wrecked by sadness, anger, and mired in sin

I cried with you
Tears not for me, but only for you
And for what you've gone through

When you cried
The hate in me died
And love came alive

I sobbed for your grief
and not my own
I cried for you and you alone

When you cried
I caught a vivid glimpse of your pain
And what mattered remained

Cry baby cry
Let the tears flow till they run dry

daughters

The voices of my daughters are joyous!
The voices of my daughters are victorious!

The voices of my daughters ring like church bells
    on a Sunday morn!
The voices of my daughters sing the everlasting
    song of those who have been reborn.

The voices of my daughters rise above the
    world's din.
The voices of my daughters proclaim war and
    victory over sin!

The voices of my daughters mingle with mine.
They speak truth, power, and love divine.

Daughters: Your voices are heard.
Your victory in me is completely assured.

diminish

You just try to diminish me.
Through your worldly ways and scornful gaze.
And break me into pieces.
With innuendo and murmuring lies,
All veiled, under your careful disguise.

I dare you to stand over me proud and tall.
Your view from on high, your downfall.
You do not get to declare my value.
Your currency worthless, measured by gain.
Too concerned with building your empire
    of sand
To truly understand.

To diminish me only makes you so very small
While I become stronger through it all.

My worth not derived from your rewritten
    history
No, it's all right here, deep within me.
You attempt to reduce me to nothing—
I'll become something!

Not because of my need to prove
But now, thanks to you, I've nothing to lose.

I'm bent, not broken,
Through the words you have spoken.
Pound your strong fist and weak will,
Go ahead, lessen me.
I'll be greater still.

empty

Empty heart
Empty hands
Here I stand

Nowhere to run
Cannot hide
Within my fear
Behind my pride

I come to your
Empty tomb
Empty cross
Where all hope seems lost

It is in the emptiness of my soul
Where I can be made whole

In the darkness of my mind
Light can shine

When I have reached the end
I can begin again

An empty cup
Completely full

even in babylon

Teach me how to live in the blessing of the now

It's been a long time waiting and anticipating
Looking back to what may never be
Right here, right now I have a new future made
    to bless me, my family and my legacy

For even in Babylon, in this lonely exile and
    foreign place
I can live in grace

Though I continue to hope for a brighter
    tomorrow in the midst of all my sorrow
Today I will begin to build on the ruins of
    the past
And my spirit will become strong and steadfast

For even in Babylon I can seize the day
And create a brand new way
I will plant, water, and watch my gardens grow
Because I know

Even in Babylon
Far from my true home
I can prosper and thrive
For I am not alone

Here I'll bring forth a bountiful harvest out of
    ashes and stony ground
For even in Babylon
In this place where all seems lost, You, God,
    can still be found

fix me

Don't try to fix me
It just won't work

You'll make me more broken
Than I was
Why can't you just love me for me, just because

I didn't ask for or want a repairman
Don't be my handy on-call man

Because you know what's wrong
With my heart
As if I'm machine and you can replace a part
To fix me all up, good as new
It'll make it easier on you

If I just run right most of the time
Then I can be yours, and you can be mine

Don't trouble you with my daily imperfection
I got news for you—You're not here to give me
    direction

I can find my own way through this life
I'm not supposed to be a perfect person or a
    perfect wife

It's not your job to fix or improve
So everything runs seamless and smooth

Messy, broken pieces on the ground
Creates chaos all around

Accept me, broken as I am
And love me even more than you think you can

forgiveness

༺

The record of wrongs
Is so very long
Kept against me
Held against you.

A long list of dids and didn't dos
Held against me
And unleashed over you.

How can that long list of wrongs be erased,
 be gone?
What kind of love keeps no record of wrongs?
How can this love even exist, and have no list?

I don't have that love
Neither do you

A God-like love
A Divine approach
To take away every error, failure, wrong word,
 and reproach

"YOU DID THIS TO ME!"
"I DID THAT TO YOU."

Checks and balances made each day, in every
　　　imaginable way.
A line-by-line accounting of our humanness.
We always stay in the red
What dread.

Never enough love in this joint account to wipe
　　　the mounting debt away
So the distance increases day after day.

Black Friday—Come!
The blackest of all days.
When all sin was accounted for and forever
　　　wiped away.
That black Friday when all hope seemed lost
Where the largest deposit of love was made.

My account now covered in blood-red,
Filled up to overflowing with forgiveness.
Yours too.

So when the record of wrongs appear
We stand before God and one another,
　　　completely in the clear.

No debt to be paid
No accounting of our sin
Instead, all nailed to Him.

Every single error, failure, wrong word,
    and reproach
now covered in blood.

That never-ending list still exists.

I can point to it.
So can you.

But when I do,
I unfurl the red-blood banner of the cross
And that list is forever gone and forever lost.

God, I bring You all my wrongs.
And all the wrongs done against me.

And I look up to that tree
Blood dripping down
From Your thorns and Your crown.

And that forgiveness covers me
From all the wrongs done to You and done
    to me.

fought and found

We yelled, we screamed
We ranted and raved

Crashing waves of fury
Pounding fists on the table

We finally said it all
No safety net to catch our fall

Laid it all out there, raw and bare.

The pulsating rhythm of anger
Drummed its steady beat

From every direction
We were assaulted and assailed
By our own confessions and secret admissions

Seconds, minutes, hours
At last—drained of all our power
We sat quietly, and you asked me to recall

And I began to remember why
Through curtains of tears
recounting one good thing after another

Afterward, you warmed my cold hands with
    your own
By the kitchen sink

My heart melted at your touch.
It was enough.

I felt close to you.
Because we fought and found our way through.

Maybe it's not about not fighting
But being able to love and to repair
Even when the fighting is not fair

fully known

Fully known
Completely owned
Not tethered between two places
But finally at home
Accepted, loved, seen

No more of this in-between
There, sitting in the lap of infinite love
In my own eternal resting place
In a room made just for me
Where I daily see God's face
This is my everlasting praise and place
Made possible by your unmerited favor
    and grace

gift of faith

∽

No present underneath the tree.
Just the gift of faith from You to me.
Enough to last the whole year through.
To lift me up when I'm feeling blue.

Don't need anything
No sweaters, toys, or diamond rings.

Just a gift of faith from You to me.
Enough to last the whole year through.
To lift me up when I'm feeling blue.

Don't need a new car or stocking stuff.
Just the gift of faith when times get rough.
Enough to last the whole year through.
To lift me up when I'm feeling blue.

Don't need the latest fad
Just a gift of faith will make me glad
Enough to last the whole year through
To lift me up when I'm feeling blue.

Wrap me up in Your arms of love
Give me faith that's from above
Enough to last the whole year through
To lift me up when I'm feeling blue.

When I get up on Christmas Morn
Give me a faith that's been reborn.
Not waiting underneath the tree
But living right inside of me.
Faith to last my whole life through
To lift me up to be near You.

good news now

I need some good news now.
Turn on the TV—CNN, FOX, CBS, ABC
What do I see?
Lyin', cheatin', schemin'
It's enough to send you screamin'

I need some Good News now
Telling me how
I'm not alone
That you're still a good God and ruling on
    the throne.
Lovin' me like a brother, better than a mother.
Closer than a friend, there 'til the end.

I need some Good News now.
Not the kind that brings me low
Tellin' me things I don't need to know.

I need some Good News TODAY, not the G the
    M or the A.
Not the N, the B, the C.
Not the F, the O, The X
But the J-E-S-U-S

I need The Good News now
About the Truth, the Way, the Life.

Tell me about His Divine Power to take away all
 this strife.
I don't need you to post that you had a fight
Being mean, hiding out behind your computer
 screen.
I need to know He'll make this wrong all right.

I need some Good News now
Telling me how
I'm not alone
That you're a powerful, kind God and You're
 ruling on the throne.
Lovin' me like a brother, better than a mother.
Closer than a friend, there until the end.

I need some Good News now
Not the TV Anchor spewing out all the rancor
What am I gonna do about it?
All it does is drag me to the pit.
So, why you keep tellin' me all this S—T?
The DOW is low, the sky is falling
What we gonna do with the name-calling?

So shut up and tell me something I really need
 to know
Like telling me how
I'm not alone
That there is a God and He's ruling on
 the throne.
Lovin' me like a brother, better than a mother.
Closer than a friend, there until the end.

Good News now
Give me the Good News now.
I don't know how.
Just need the good, Good News now.

how do you say goodbye to your mother?

***

How do you say goodbye to your mother?
You don't.
You are a part of her and she of you.
Carried within her womb; blood of her blood,
    flesh of her flesh.

Closer than a sister, lover, or a brother
Are children and their mothers.

You are hers, yet still in and of yourself,
    your own.
A child then, an adult now: All grown.

How do you say goodbye to your mother?
You don't.
Instead, you look in the mirror each new day—
And you say,
"Good morning, Mom. The best of you is carried
    deep within me."

You see her reflection in yourself—at different
    times and in every place.
The way you tilt your head, your laugh,
    your voice.
As if you had no choice!

Your own physical and emotional assent
Shaped and bent
By her idiosyncrasies and personal proclivities
Me in her and her in me.

Within and without.
There leaves no doubt.
I am my mother's. Forever.

How do I say goodbye to my mother?
I never will. I won't.
I go on and she goes on in me.
My Mother's Love. No ending and no start.
Held right here, forever and always, in her son
    and daughter's hearts.

i asked you to leave

I asked you to leave
But I want you to stay

Because us being together gets in the way
Too much pain and not enough gain

I want you to stay
But I asked you to leave
Because I want us to breathe

I need to be me, to be free from the day to day
To find a new way

This air is heavy and not light
As we daily rumble and fight

I asked you to leave cause my mind says go
I want you to stay, cause my heart says no

Too many years to just let it all disappear
Without you here
Without you near
I want you to leave
But I'm asking you to stay

i choose joy

Cause there's joy down in the valley of all my fears.
Joy in the midst of all my tears.

This I know for sure.
In You I am secure.
So let the world shake.
Let the fakers fake.
My faith may sway and quake.
But it will not break.

'Cause I choose Joy down in the valley.
Hope to lift me up.
Peace as my crown.
Nothin's gonna bring me down.

Jesus, You're gonna right the wrong.
And I will come to find.

Joy down in the valley of all my fears.
Joy in the midst of all my tears.

I choose Joy in the valley.
Hope to lift me up.
Peace as my crown.
Nothin's gonna bring me down

Jesus, You're gonna right the wrong.
No doubt.
You're gonna straighten it all out.

i keep remembering you

○○○

I will remember You
Through it all

As I fail and fall
I will recall

Who You are
Have always been
Even when
I do not know my way
Tomorrow or today

As I question
What I don't understand
I'll take hold of Your hand
Turn my face to Your face
And, I'll keep remembering You

On Your holy hill
As I desire to do Your will

At Your altar
As I flail and falter

I'll remember who You are
Have always been

Will forever be
To me
The God who cares
El, transcendent, always there

I'll keep remembering You
Through it all
In Your dwelling place
When I see Your face
There, and in every time and place,
I will remember You.

in the grey

God is in the grey
In the vast unknown
And the everyday

We like to make Him black or white
To hide our gnawing fear and fright
So that we constantly argue and fight
Over who's wrong and who's right

But I will pause to recall
That God is over all

And when I do not know my way
I know that God is in the grey

We like to make Him red, white, and blue
To divide me and you

But He is greater than any one nation
Far above every government, people, and tribe
God is there to unify
Not to divide

So let us remember today
That God is in the grey

He is in the chaos
And in the calm

To do us each good and not harm

in the meanwhile

I know that you are here with me
Between the devil and the deep blue sea

Please do not leave me on this shore
Wondering and waiting anymore

This in-between is slowly killing me
Rescue me and part this sea

I know you are with me in the meanwhile.

But I don't understand
The work of your hand

Why won't you do something to move me on
    through this trial
As I walk another weary mile

If this middle is a riddle
That I cannot solve
I have lost all my resolve

Bring me to that promised land You
    promised me.
Part the sea!

Do this for me!
And swallow up my enemy

Lead me through on dry ground
Make a way where none can be found
Create a wall of water
Move me on so that my feet no longer falter

I'm so tired of standing here
Waiting for You to appear
As my enemy keeps drawing near

Do something now between the devil and the
 deep blue sea
For me and for my family
So I can tell the story
Of Your amazing grace and glory

last kiss

Your last, lingering kiss
Will grant me my lifelong hope and everlasting
 wish:

To kiss the Face brighter than the stars and sun
To whom my soul has been tethered and where
 my heart is won

For the last kiss here
Will be my first kiss there

So let me kiss your lips goodbye
As I am raised on high

Your final kiss for me
Means that I will finally be
Where this horizon meets my sweet and
 everlasting destiny

On that day I will be free from death and decay
As a welcoming army of angels greet me with
 song, dance, and play.

So grant me this last kiss and my final wish
Press your lips softly and sweetly on mine
So I can be eternally entwined with the Divine

living grief

This living grief swallows up the other grief
That I should be allowed to feel, so that I
    can heal

It is monstrous—insatiable in its hunger to steal
    every hope and each moments joy
It is a crashing wave that doesn't abate nor wait
    for the in and out of the tide
No. It keeps pounding and pounding me from
    every side.
Until it's pushed me far under its crushing
    weight
Intent to kill me with hopelessness and hate

Even when I struggle up for air
It is still there

Screeching at me
From the depths of the sea

"God doesn't care
He is not there"

"There's nothing you can do nor pray
That will change this, keep it at bay or remove it
    far away"

I am drowning in this angry sea of rolling grief
It has taken all, this loathsome thief
There has been no calm nor sweet relief

I thought you promised me these things:
Hope, Peace, Joy
Or was it all a Divine ploy?

I just didn't realize then, but I do now
That these comforting companions only show up
After I've been ripped apart
Bone by bone
Left alone
And utterly destroyed
By grief and doubt
From the inside out.

more

Still searching for that perfect place to call home
    and rest your head
When you find it, will you lie awake upon
    your bed
And wonder, is there more out there for me?

Desperate for that perfect girl or guy
When you find them will you still come home
    and say
Is there more out there for me?

Fantasizing through the screen
When it's not really real, not what it seems

Dreaming of your next great flight
Land on that distant shore
See the sights and come back home
Then it's all over, it's all done

But your soul's still yearning for that great quest
When all it really needs is peace and rest
Is there more out there for me?

Not outside your home
Not some far offshore
Not the boy next door

There is more for you
A life of peace
The hope of Heaven

Sins forgotten
All forgiven
The more you're searching for

Not outside your door
But right here, right now
Knocking on your heart

Let more come in
A life of peace
The hope of Heaven
Sins forgotten
All forgiven

morning rush

Yelling, "Kids get in the car!"
We don't have to drive too far
First to school, then to work on time
This crazy life of mine.

Quiet hush
What is that?
I've been meaning to get to You, just can't.

Morning rush
"Get up, get going," we cajole and rant
I've been meaning to get to You, just can't.

Lord, here's a minute of my day
Can't wait to hear what You'll say.

I've been meaning to get to know You more,
but just not now.
I'll be back, I swear to God.
Right now, I've got to work out on this bod.

And then pick up something at the store.
I've been meaning to get to know You more,
But just not now, I can't.

End of day, dishes done
Crawl to bed, rest my head
Quiet now
I'm lulled to sleep.
And then You speak.

"I love you
In the morning rush
In the minutes stolen
In the quiet hush
No matter where you are, at any time
I love you child
because you're mine."

on the day i was born

On the day I was born
I had everything I needed
A mother and a father to love me and provide,
    a brother and sisters by my side

On the day I was born
I had everything
Trust and a love to hold and keep me safe
The gift of new life and grace
A tender heart, a warm embrace

On the day I was born
I was loved for just being here and just being me
For just being

On the day I was born again
I had everything I needed
A Father to love me, the Holy Spirit to guide and
    provide, Jesus my friend—and sisters and
    brothers by my side
On the day I was born again
I had everything
Trust and a love to hold and keep me safe
A tender heart, a warm embrace
The gift of new life and grace

On the day I was born again
I was loved for just being here and just being me
For just being

On the day of my birthday
I have everything I need
Friends and family, my daughters and a son to
    love and guide, my husband, and sisters and
    brothers by my side
I have everything.
Trust and love to hold and keep me safe
A tender heart, a warm embrace
The gift of life and grace

On the day of my birthday
I have everything I need
Within and without, standing right in front
    of me

On the day of my birthday
I am loved for just being here and just being me
For just being.

Happy Birthday to me.
Because of Him, because of you
I am loved. I am safe. I am free.

Happy Birthday to me.

outside the gate

Left behind
Not a friend to rely on nor to find

For twenty years we fought side by side
to help keep the flame of freedom alive.

You gave up, gave in and gifted our mortal
    enemy with storehouses full of murderous
    machinery.

They've plundered it all
Made us kowtow and fall
Jubilant dancers roam blood-stained streets
    celebrating their victory and our shameful
    departure of defeat

You turned out the lights
Slipped away in the middle of the night
Up and walked away
Without a parting punch or fight

"Too tired," you say
We just don't care enough to stay
a few days more
To make sure we return to loving arms
or new welcoming shores

We are left standing
outside the gate
While you fly up and away
To live another day

Too late.
So we and all the world will wait
For the harbingers of hate
To seal our shared fate

put the stone down

Put the stone down
Set it on the ground
Go on and walk away
It's a brand new day

No more pointing fingers and sharp stones
A grace never before known
Is here to show you the way home

It's just you and me, alone and safe
Eye to eye
Face to face
Lift your gaze to the King of amazing grace

It's a brand new day
Never again to pay
You will not die today
For love has made the way

Put the stone down
Set it on the ground
See, they've all walked away
It's a brand new day

These stones will cry out and be rolled away
On my soon and coming Resurrection Day.

Grace has freed you from the laws of men
Opened wide the gates of Heaven

These heavy stones are forever put away
Yesterday, tomorrow, and today.
For Love will take your place
On the cross of grace

railroad tracks

Railroad tracks, parallel lines
Going nowhere at the same time

You keep on your side,
I'll keep on mine

I don't need you nor want you on my track
Stay off my path and get off my back

Do what you do, day-to-day
Just don't get in my way

I don't care enough about you to cross the line
You keep on your side
I'll keep on mine

Railroad tracks, parallel lines
Going nowhere at the same time

We'll arrive at our destination
Our designated station

Mangled rail weary cars ripped apart
And then we'll once again depart

I'm doing just fine on my side of the tracks
Don't look over, don't look back

Keep on chugging and plugging away
Do what you do, day-to-day
Just don't get in my way
Don't cross the line

Because I'm doing all right all alone over here.
    I'm fine.

remarkable

He came home to us on Memorial Day after
    years of being away
He said he was just stopping by for a short stay

As he made plans to reach that ancient shore
I was glad he was here with us once more

I knew he wouldn't be here much longer
He was growing weaker, not stronger

With his bright blue eyes and smile
I begged my dad to stay and linger here with us
    a while

I sat with him as his years were coming to a close
And wondered why he chose the paths he chose

He looked straight in my direction
With fatherly affection said
"You're a remarkable woman
You've been an amazing daughter.
No dad on earth could have asked for any more
    than what you've given me.
Now it's time to set my spirit free"

And my questions didn't matter anymore
Because my dad had said the words I had been
    waiting my life for
That I'm his remarkable daughter
I've been his faithful friend

As he breathed his final breath
I sat with him and held him close to me
Enveloped in our own history

And my questions didn't matter anymore
Because my dad had said the words I had been
    waiting my whole life for
That I'm his remarkable daughter
I've been an amazing friend

Now I sit with my children, missing him, and
    when I do
I whisper his words to myself
I'm a remarkable woman
I've been his faithful friend

And I look up at him and say
"You've been a remarkable father, a faithful
    friend
No daughter on earth could have asked for any
    more than what you've given me
Now it's time for me to set your spirit free"

run into hope

I'll run into hope
And push through the pain

I've nothing to lose
And everything to gain

So, I'm going in to see
What Jesus will do for me

Leaving my shame and failures far behind
A risen Lord and forever friend to find

No standing back and lingering outside
I'm going in and putting aside
My fear, doubt, and pride

And there, in the deep and the darkened tomb
My heart will make room
For hope to rebloom

sabbatical

A true rest to find the truest rest
A long, heart-breaking break from the constant
    scurrying,
And ever-present worrying
Pieces of my soul made whole.
Is *one day* enough to set aside.
To take refuge from life's landslides.

Today, I ponder all that is grace and beauty
A privilege, a gift, a wondrous, sacred duty
Every day—a Sabbath.
For truth, love and hope to spring up
Where heart and mind are allowed to take a spell
Right here, right now, where I daily live
    and dwell
Work, job, title no longer to compel

I drink thirstily from this ever-flowing cup
Each moment now … a pleasant pause, to linger
    a little longer
Here, racing thoughts take their ease
All that ails is ushered out, forced to take
    its leave
One day. Every day. Each moment.

To strengthen what is weak, set right what
    is wrong.
Weary, worried, wounded
Refreshed, renewed, revived
Stopped. To start again.
To be reawakened to life.
In order to live fully alive.

shoreline

Strong winds, furious waves
Batter me
Yet here I stand
My feet affixed on rock
Not sand

A billion particles swirl about me
Yet here I stand
Legs strong
Back upright
Safely held by an unseen hand

Storms will come
The sea will rise and fall
Yet I will stand
Through it all

Heart, soul, spirit—finally yielded
To the great unknown
It shows me the way home
Home is here, where I Am

"Bludgeon Me,"
I scream to the sea
"Do everything you can

To get me to fall and not stand
Take it all
Job, hearth and home"

For I will stand
But not alone

stay

I stayed.

I didn't go.
To the black hole

Oh, I had a thousand thoughts of him
    down there.
Alone and unaware.

With the television screen blaring
Surrounded by sound, but silence abounds
caring and uncaring.

I stayed. Right where I was.
Because when I lingered, she was there,
    beside me.
The way it used to be.

And while I cleaned, she talked and preened.

Then, the surprising glory
"Mom, can I read you a story?"

Me with my she-girl
a priceless pearl

There was no stomping off, locking herself
    behind a closed door, leaving,
This night, only cleaving.

A second question beckons,
"Mom, can I come to your room tonight?"

Up we went.
And we both lay down to write

Mother and daughter
Sharing our story, our worlds, our words.
Paper and pen
Together again.

Good Night.

ten thousand decrees

One official divorce decree issued by you
To equal the 10,000 divorce decrees I served
Year over year
Week on week
Day after day
When I didn't like what you didn't do or
 didn't say
Or when I just didn't get my way

One heavy sheaf of lawyered documents
A response to the frustrated verbal crumbs I left
 along the way
Threatened to leave, to depart
When you couldn't, just wouldn't answer the cry
 of a wounded, rejected heart

Barbed-wired notes strewn carelessly about
 our home
Scrawled out loud that I'd rather be with
 someone else, or maybe just alone

Daggers of divorce decrees issued straight to
 your soul and heart
Tearing you and us bit by bit apart
A growling paper lion roared and roared
Was cajoled, appeased, and eventually ignored

Every single piece you angrily and sadly
 tucked away
Inside yourself, inside your head
You believed what I said

Woke up each morning with the weight,
 the dread
Will this be the day when I get served
With threatening words and insults absurd?

Through the years, collected all those divorce
 decrees, remembered every one
And decided for now and for forever that
 I'm done
I've finally spoken
Hear me loud and clear
My lover whom I once held dear...
"Irretrievably broken"
That's what I'll say

Stamped and signed via paper and ink
I've heard ten thousand times what she thinks.
Taken us here, to the brink.
And so, I finally and reluctantly agree
With the 10,000 verbal decrees
That came my way
Week on week
Day after day

that girl

I want to be that girl in the world
That girl that was before in Australia, Brazil,
    Italy, DC
Ready for You to use me
Hungry for Your presence
Bold and confident

I want to be that girl in this world
Relying on You alone
Not on a man, children, job, or my home
A grown woman now,
Make me that girl again.

The one that was always ready to stand and
    defend
The one that wanted to serve and love
    without end
And would go wherever You would lead me
Fearless and unafraid of the future, the next day
I have lost my way

Knowing I was sharing in Your glory, writing
    another chapter in Your story
That shared Your love to strangers near and far
What happened to that girl?
Who believed You could do anything

I have lost my way
In the day to day

Lost girl now
That girl then
Help me to begin again

the better part

The better part—heals my heart
The better part—a new start

Sitting in this pain hurts too much.
I'd rather be doing something other
Then the better part:
Accomplishing
Winning
Checking off another list
Reaching my goal
You see—this is what makes me, me.
Whole.

To do that which can be easily seen
Will mean
Recognition, celebration
To shout, "Look at all I've done!"

I'm winning a race that can never be won.

It puts a smile on my face
To keep up this crazy pace

But the smile quickly fades.
There is always more to do
An endless list of endless tasks

I love this busy life I've made
It keeps me from being afraid.
My to-dos, a barrier I've built from me to you.
They help me hide behind my mask

Besides, what will I really gain
By acknowledging my pain?

Harder still is to sit still
To listen, to be held and sheltered by love
To experience the endless thrill
Of what can never be taken away
The internal eternal, each and every day.

This race—it's all I know and where I thrive
Oh, it's the perfect place where I come alive.
These tasks, they gladly pull me away
Into doing for another day.

Not having to face the real reason for this
    driving pace
That I, like you, desperately need unending grace

The invitation that says, "Come sit down for just
    a little while."
You'll have many reasons to smile

It will heal your hurting heart
From the inside out.

To just stop.
The better part.
It's a brand new start.

The best you that you can be
Waiting to be revealed
Is found in sitting here with me.

the exchange

I empty myself of all I hold dear
So I can hear

I choose to become less
So I can hold more

I empty myself
Of myself and open wide the door

"Come in, come in"
I invite You into my heart
The inmost part

I empty myself of myself
So I can be full

Keeper of my life
Lover of my soul
I empty myself of my self
So I can be whole

tired

I'm tired of crying
I'm tired of trying
I'm tired of on the inside dying

I'm weary of this war
I don't want this anymore

I'm tired of failing
I'm tired of prevailing

I'm weary of this fight
In the morning, in the evening, and at night

I'm tired of the mournful dance and song
Of proving which one of us is wrong
And which one of us is right

I'm tired.
Let me sleep.
Sleep this all away

Until tomorrow, another day
When we get to press repeat.
And do this all over again

Can't we find another path
That doesn't have the aftermath
Of the constant power struggle
That has become a life
Filled full of strife

Point and shame
Blame and accuse
So neither one of us has to lose.
We'll win the battle but not the war
And lose everything else
In the quest to gain ourselves.

All alone with our proving and pride
Has it already been decided
That this love is not worth the high cost?
Because right now, it all seems lost

to be vulnerable

Truth in the inmost part
a flashlight into the heart

To understand and speak from deep within
To move forward despite the fear

To know yourself enough
To be able to reveal your thoughts
In a way that is raw and unafraid

To know no matter what I say
Or what may come
What may be done or undone
I have spoken from my heart of hearts

Though it may tear me apart
On the outside
I am healed
On the inside
By what I have revealed

My heart, my inmost thoughts, my soul
By being truly vulnerable
Unafraid
Miraculously, I am made whole

upside-down

My world has turned upside-down
And I am about to bottom out and go
    underground.
All so crazy and curvy
Not right side up, but topsy-turvy

What happened to a life straight and narrow
Like a bow and arrow
How does all this trouble and woe
Lead me to a good and lasting goal.

We can find peace in the upside-down
Gain treasure in our heavenly crown
Breathe in serenity and not drown

Because You, God, are in this lonely, terrifying
    place
Our safety in this not-safe space

A light so powerful that we can see
Through this shrouded misery

In the upside-down
All hope seems lost
At far too great a cost

We will hear Love calling out if we stop
    and search
Waiting to find and gift us with divine power
    and spiritual rebirth.

Bring me to You
For a brand new perspective and view
I can still be right side up here in the
    upside-down
Knowing everything doesn't have to be in order
    for You to still be true

waterfall

I've cried a million tears
I've faced a thousand fears

I've sat in my loneliness and pain
What have I gained?

A battered, bruised heart and soul
Feeling half, not whole
Emptied of all I once held dear
Makes it all crystal clear:

That living is a hard-fought battle
And victory appears an unattainable goal
That shouldering the heavy load of loving
Is too much for any one soul
That this cannot be done alone

"I AM with you"
"I am with YOU"
I hear my strong brother say
"I am WITH you"
Yesterday, tomorrow, and this day

I'll fight on your behalf
Sit back and just relax
I've got this one

Sweet friend of mine,
For I am human and divine

You are too tired to pick up sword and shield
In me, your victory is assured

I understand what you face
I know how to run this race
My power greater than all of your fears
My love captures and keeps your waterfall
    of tears

we shared scars

We shared scars
An accident in a VW bus
A year of gourmet family dinners, morning
    coffee and tea, just us.

Marigolds in dirt
Matching polyester pant suits with multi-colored
    shirts

We shared beds and rooms
Tompkins street chores, cleaning stairs, and
    mopping floors

Gas-pump pretend play
In a New York village far away

Tadpole fishing in the creek
Summer day camp, boondoggling all week

Walks to the Lemon Drop
Sharing doughnuts and candy until we popped

Waking up on a Sunday morning
Our bikes, the bright orange VW, all gone—
    without warning

The repo men came and took it all away, that
    bright and sunny day

We shared elementary and middle schools
The same teachers, crushes on boys, and the
    nun's rules.

We shared God's grace
When you said yes to life and love in a Syracuse
    church
Your place of spiritual rebirth

We shared a love of lyric and rhyme
We gave each other the gift of time

We shared unrecoverable loss
Rushing you to our dad to say our final
    goodnight
After a long, transatlantic flight

We shared affection for our ancestral home
We traveled north, south, east, and west
But agreed, Italy was the best.

We shared dreams
No matter what and through it all
We held on to our unbreakable sister bond
Rejoicing in victories, great or small
And catching each other in the fall

We shared short and long telephone calls,
    connecting us through the miles
As we waded deep into life's storms and trials

We shared prayers full of desperate pleas for
    ourselves and our families

We had each others back when the enemy of our
    souls went on the attack

We shared our final sister trip, traipsed through
    gardens scented with roses and mountain air
You walked miles in the heat, pressing through
    and not missing a beat
You were happy to be alive and just there

We shared pain and tears, joys and sorrows
Hope for each other's brighter tomorrows

We shared God's glory
We were each other's chapters in a lifelong
    sister story

Forever written in our hearts
Is the love we shared as sisters and friends from
    the start

Our lives and love are bound and entwined
    through days and decades of time.

what if

༄

What if all the uninvited "What ifs" constantly
    elbowing into my thoughts day by day
Found another way to say

What if?

What if it's

NOT Cancer
NOT the end of this marriage
NOT a dead-end job
NOT substance abuse
NOT a wayward daughter or son
NOT I'll always be alone
NOT I'll never be at peace or feel at home
NOT financial ruin
NOT family dysfunction

What if the "What if" is good, pleasing, more
And even better than before?

What if the "What if" is joyous and greater than
    my wildest imaginings?

What if the "What ifs" of my darkened, doubting mind
Fell into line with the goodness, mercy, and love of the Divine

What if I wholly trusted God in the what ifs

Leaving them all laying scattered and littered on the ground
Trampled into dust by a trust more powerful than the sum of all my fears
Running into and held by the everlasting arms that keep me safe and sound
What if?

when dreams sleep

When dreams sleep
When deep desires are slowly silenced
Wishes go ungranted and promises unkept
And you feel alone—and left

What do you do
When your dreams fade away into the starry night
And don't awake with the morning light

Do you give up or give over
Surrender or fight

When dreams sleep
Do you sit and weep
Or stand and defend

When dreams sleep
Are they resting for a little while
As you walk another weary mile
Until you reach the end
Only to start over again

When dreams sleep
Are they being re-created in you
So you'll awaken anew

What do you do
While your dreams sleep-away
And you must face another day
Dreamless and awake
Longing for your dreams to be revived
So you live wholly alive

Can you live without a dream being realized
And still be you while you struggle and wait
Or are you the constant companion to envy,
    bitterness, and hate

Old dreams, you can stay fast asleep.
I'll day-dream you far away
And dream a new dream today

I'll cry, weep, shake my fist, then stand and
    defend
And I'll do it over and over again
Day after day, sorrow upon sorrow

Until my new dream wakes up and becomes
    reality—one day

Maybe tomorrow.

wish you were here

Where you are, there are endless days full of
 glorious wonder.
We are here, ticking off days, months and years,
 marveling at the roaring sound of thunder.
Where we sit, here upon the world's rim,
We strain to see you, your visage cast in
 memory's shadow, growing even more dim.

We are bound by flesh, sun, and sky.
Even now we stand upon this weary earth,
 asking, "Why?"
You are where days are endless and unceasing.
We are here where trouble and worry advance
 incessantly, constantly increasing.

You are where the healing balm has been
 irrevocably applied.
You are where time is no longer bound by
 measure.
We are here, seeking heavenly and earthly
 treasure.
We are here, marching to the tick tock of
 our clocks.
Where time sneers and mocks.

You are there, fully realized in truth and love.
We are here, in the shadowlands, struggling betwixt faith and fear.
Waiting for our own eternal awakening.
"Precious sister, daughter, friend—We wish you were here."
And you, over on that distant shore, say our name and whisper the very same words in our ear.

worlds upon worlds

There are worlds upon worlds deep within you
That have yet to be born and formed
These worlds are made of words, fantastical
    thoughts and wondrous deeds
They are birthed in a mind of infinite
    possibilities
And from a heart untroubled by worldly woes
This I know:
These worlds that you create
Will be both powerful and great
For they were forged from within the fires of
    your own doubt and pain
Held in you by a strength eternal and divine
Outside of space and time
There are worlds roiling beneath the surface of
    the sea
Tremors of thoughts and shrouded mysteries
Waiting to burst forth into majestic and verdant
    scenery
For all to wonder and see
So, my son, go forth to establish your worlds in
    the hearts of men
Yielding not a sword, but a pen.

wounded womb

Hope died within the day you were taken
> from me.

My womb, blessed with your presence too
> briefly; then quickly and savagely stolen
> away that unwelcome unbirthday.

The day my womb became your tomb
Hope left me for a long weary season and time.
Will what I want so dearly ever become mine?

Sadness subside, be gone your treacherous
> thieving.
For I will one day walk beyond this grieving.

I speak to hope—gently, quietly bloom inside my
> aching heart
Yield your fruit within my wounded womb.
And bring forth life out of this tomb.

write don't fight

If we picked up pens
Instead of swords
And let our words roar

Using prose and poetry
Ink and pen
To settle every score
Between mice and men

To seek what is within
Before we ever begin
Making ourselves right
To raise up arms to fight
If we wrote instead of warred

Allowing the word
To wreak havoc on our own souls first
Armed now with thoughtful reflection
Instead of harmful rejection

If we wrote first
The hardest battle is then already fought
    and won
And no more fighting need be done

wrong made right

When life goes every which way wrong
Our faith, our trust, and we ourselves fumble through, and then we grow mighty and strong.

We ask for blessing and peace, a life free from wounds, hurt, and pain.
But it is only through the heavy trial that we gain.

If you hadn't decided once again to shoulder love's load
If your lives had taken a different road
We wouldn't be standing here celebrating this undeniable truth:
That God is able to revive and restore, to make our love and lives better than they were before.

We look at you with new eyes in this new place
For you are a masterfully retouched portrait of mercy and grace.
Because of you, we believe that God Himself can right any wrong.
And carry us through any storm, to a safe port where hope is reborn.

Because of you we know without a doubt
That no one and nothing is ever too far from
    God's hand to reach.
Your lives, your marriage, a daily lesson does
    us teach.
That when wrongs are made right

We each shine brighter through the night
And awake with the new dawn in Christ's
    glorious light.

about the author

Jeannine Gibson epitomizes the modern-day Renaissance woman—one day penning pages of poetry, the next in her career role as a marketing and branding executive. A typical day in her storied career would find her tending to every detail in arranging a massive professional event or conference, or planning various soirees for friends and family, as connecting people with each other and with their Divine purpose is her joy.

Whether writing from the heart, enjoying time with her family and beloved German shepherd, Teddy, or focused on professional pursuits, she approaches every action with passion and purpose. Her poetry is inspired by her family, her surroundings, and her perspective on life experiences that have profoundly impacted her, and those nearest and dearest to her.

A graduate of the University of Rochester, native of Syracuse, New York, and the middle child of a large Italian-American family, Jeannine has called Northern Virginia home for over three decades after her clunker of a car broke down on Route 66 inside the beltway.

She is available to share her poems and the stories that inspired them with your group or organization.